'Ware Yourself: memories of pain, Joy and hope

Mark James

BookLeaf Publishing

India | USA | UK

'Ware Yourself: memories of pain, Joy and hope © 2021 Mark James

All rights reserved.

No part of this publication may be reproduced, stored in a retrieval system, or transmitted, in any form or by any means, electronic, mechanical, photocopying, recording or otherwise, without the prior written permission of the presenters.

Mark James asserts the moral right to be identified as author of this work.

Presentation by *BookLeaf Publishing*

Web: www.bookleafpub.com

E-mail: info@bookleafpub.com

ISBN : 9789357447218

First edition 2021

DEDICATION

To all the people that inspire me to try, but
always for Dean, River, and Zoey.

ACKNOWLEDGEMENT

I'm not sure if the remodeling on the surface of my grey matter after the concussion, or the terror, love, and care I recieved from a friend are to blame for my return to this medium of expression.

PREFACE

Anything worth doing is worth doing poorly, but
there is no such thing as poorly done art.

Just let go

Let it go
You can't heal until you let it go
There's no time limit
Take your time
You'll just hurt until you let it go

Let it go
You can't heal until you let it go
There are other worlds
It was just your life
You'll keep hurting until you let it go

Let it go
You can't heal
Hurry up
I won't wait
You'll keep hurting
Until you let it go

Until you let it go

Nihilist

Scream until your voice breaks
Scream to drown out the world

Acknowledge your fear
Feel your pain

No one hears you
No one cares

You're a hero now
I can't do this anymore

Failing in love

How do you quit?
I'm broken, I'm hurt, I'm tired
Everything I do is right, but it's not enough
There must have been a time I didn't struggle
When was the last time there wasn't a fight?
Fight your feelings
Fight disease
Fight yourself
Every day fall down seven, get up eight
Little eyes watch unknowing
Little hearts are full of love
Fight to be there: lose
Fight for your rights: lose
Fight the feeling you're not enough: lose
Fight to quit: fail
Little hands lift you up
Fight the tears: fail
Little voices say it's okay, we got you daddy
Massive hugs from little bodies
All I do is fail, but With those little eyes on my I
cannot quit
Little voices say I love you daddy

Tarot 1

Cards flipped into a vague arc
    Runner, your a runner
More cards flipped
    Your going to run from me
So sad, she thinks I'm at a stop

Really you are just in my wake
    Running as far as I can
Why would you run away
    It's not running from you
So sad, she thinks I'm at a stop

I ran as far as I could
    Bummer bummer bummer
It was never enough to escape
    Completely unrelated to you
So sad, I don't think I can actually stop

Afterthought

Treated as an afterthought, an inconvenience on
a good day, my name is you're not a regret

Read as: accident, mistake, unintended.

But, oh so important and special so long as you
aren't costing any time, money or effort.
So special until you become even the tiniest of
inconveniences.

Unbelievable, you're so selfish, so stupid, look at
what you cost me! Everything else is more
important than you, the most important part of
my world.

The afterthought
That was a mistake.
Not a regret.
Because it has to be handled.

Fairy Tales

Getting over it is a fairy tale
Leaving behind the love that could only hit and
yell
Scars burn anew when you remember there was
nobody there
And even for the stronger better you it is too
much to bear
Shows and songs make tears course down your
face
As you are reminded of the permanent painful
haze
You have come so far from that place
you are so much stronger and hale
But getting over it is still a fairy tale

1st Haiku

There was much passion
One heart seemingly broken
One heart unbroken

2nd Haiku

Call anybody
I have lost all vital signs
There will be no shroud

Bad boy

Telling me you want a bad boy when really you just want a toy was your mistake.
James Bond and Josey Wales showed me how much grief not to take
Having both skill and charm makes you want to hang on my arm
Yet when I am too much you wish me harm
Screaming at me, never a good woman will I find
Why weren't my childhood role models in your mind?
Monster you cry
spits I was made this way watching my true love die.

Yvonne

Snow Covered Streets
Warmth and Beauty before me
Grief far behind us

Children

Six pairs of blue eyes
Light and love greater than the sun
Wisdom beyond years

Separation from Joy

Monster she calls me
Begging for my attention
Lashing out in spite

Heroic Lie

Heroes get remembered, legends never die, so
goes the old lie
Just over a year, the heroes of a pandemic are
forgotten
Before that all we knew was manipulation and
treatment that was rotten
How is it that we are surprised by the same
administration that has always lied?!
Abusers always do find the best way to take
advantage of you
Victims look for the best way to survive and
push through
It is a match made in hell, the heroes at the front,
controlled by those that
    avoided the brunt

I heard a pager buzz

I heard a pager buzz when my patient died
No stillness in the room
Reflected my still thrumming heart
No calm in this storm

Every eye stayed dry

Breathing collectively stopped
when time of death was called
Be a witness, sign the sheet

No willed keepsakes, all quarantined
None of my patients portions assignable, and
there buzzed a pager

Steady continuous vibration
between peace and she,
and then the shroud fell
no longer could we see

My first bad day

0545
Trying to make up for the man that I am, I
stopped to help.
Traffic ballooning into the breakdown lanes,
brake lights looking for all the world
　　like arterial blood.
In the time it took for me to get to the body in
the street, that brought my day to
　　a halt, another person in scrubs had
materialized.
She's doing compressions, but no one really
wants to give rescue breaths to the
　　bloody beard
There's a motorcycle up the road, most likely
his.
Salvation in the cries for help at another vehicle.
Funny how no one stuck around once the scrubs
came over.
An old man slumped in his seat, his Honda rear
ended to the size of a Yugo.
Except you do not get to go, not alone.
Taking c-spine, murmuring comfort because I
don't know if he is still there or
　　not, not wanting those respirations to be as
irregular as they seem

I watch his life leave his body.
No one is helping him, no one is helping me.
Funny, there are at least a half dozen firefighters
around now, no extrications to
    do, why is this moment stretching to eternity,
or is this just the space
    between actual respirations?
Panic sets in as I sit in a modified bus, brought
up for the volunteer first
    responders I'm running late, I make phone
calls, but suddenly the biggest
    problem I am having is not that I just
watched two people die, but that I won't
    be at clinicals on time.
Phone calls are made, and I am only just a little
late,
0746
in fact I got let in by my also late preceptor.
As a wounded animal I stubbornly continue on,
crashing through my day.
    Isn't this part of the job?
Shouldn't I be able to shake off these losses like
water off the proverbial duck?
Things look better snagging a free meal in the
break room and joking about I
    don't remember what.
Cunning Fate grabs hold of the ignored spear in
my soul, twisting with sudden
    and sadistic glee

1400
Incoming code, six weeks old.
Everyone is doing everything exactly right.
Students exceeding make terrified
    eye contact, a doctor gently talks to a tearful
mother who nods.
Intervention stops, and then there is the scream.
An infant that survived beyond her prognosis
falls asleep in her mother's arms.
No more struggle, no bells, no needles, no tubes.
Only the soft exhale, that sounds like I was here
1700
Now in a conference room, with instructors that
aren't sure what to do, with the
    legacy of growing up in a burn ICU, of
military medicine, but only just now
    really coming into heavy contact with that
arch nemesis death
Can you finish the day?
Of course, that is the job
There are only two hours left to the day anyways
1900
I got all my paperwork done. It was a hard day,
but we gotta push through right?
It isn't like you get to go home when you're
really doing the job.
See you in class tommorow.

Sorry Walt

When I hear America singing, it varies year to
year
What was pure in my youth, is now unsure
Soldiers sing as they march to and from a
senseless war
Programmers sing to accompany the staccato of
their keys as they work dusk to
    dawn, coding to keep the masses quiet
Children sing as they trudge to school, though
that tends to only be a few feet
First responders have a curious note of jollity as
they perform courageous acts
    of self sacrifice
A song of thanks breathily given by those they
save, as they are rushed out
    before the next wave
Tranquil tunes of motherhood, which stretch to
time forgot
Waitresses dance to their own music, singing as
they serve, grateful the work
    returned
Comedians make you tear with the grief of their
song

    while TV anchors make you cry from
laughter at their courtly jests
I still hear America warble, though it is hard to
catch those notes we hold so
    dear.
Keep it up, keep singing your love, loud and
clear.

Emo

Hell's gates open
  clamoring for my soul,
    for it is sick and selfish and cruel
Wait
    This must be lunacy
      surely some sort of fallacy
        have I not freely given all that I am?
          Sacrificed me, to help all of you
Perhaps I have truly sinned so mightily that
naught can save me
      No amount of sacrificce or self abasement
        now I must pass that wicked gate
All that I was and all that I did
  could not outweigh that which was wicked.
    I am not the creator, and I am not allowed
to doubt
      Questions are not tolerated, for there
is only one answer
There is no balance between what we save and
what we ruin
    You have to choose the one absolute truth
      do not worry, there is only the one
        so long as you pick it, and you do it
before time runs out

What we got

Epic love, fit for a novel or a movie, is what I
sought
A quick flash, snuffed by it's own intensity is
what I got
Desire and passion became duty and
responsibility
Pride and joy became obligation and scarcity
At what point did it all go wrong?
Sacrifice, the hallmark of epic love, was not
what I thought
Appreciation of the sacrifice, not worth what it
bought
Comfort and affection suffered from a paucity
When did we lose the magic and song?
How did our beautiful love succumb to such an
ague?
Our grand adventure was cut short, when the
American Dream became our court.

A Man

Here
Just for you
a man
Just a man
no more
no less
everything as it should be

why this one?

well let's see
he is just like all of the other men in the world.

like most he has two legs.
His two legs are unique.
They have carried him countless miles over
many countries.
These two legs have marched, and helped him to
carry those that could not carry themselves.

Similar to others of his species are his hands.
Also two of those.
This specific set has held brand new life, as well
as brand new death.

these particular hands are strong and unyielding,
while being soft and gentle and comforting

The eyes have a cool feature, they change color
with the season.
Other than superficial beauty they have seen
exquisite beauty (none quite as exquisite as you)
and grotesque horrors.

Forget that last bit. This man has pretty soulful
eyes.

Overall his body is, average. Not that it leaves
anything to be desired, there just isn't much
flash.
the scars are faded, and the tattoos are
meaningful in that deeply personal way.

Ah, but its what is under the hood that counts
eh?

Yes, the heart in this one. The heart is
indestructible.
This man's heart is full of depthless love and
compassion.
Others have stomped it, thrown it, tore at it, and
it is still whole.
where another would be bitter and awful, this
one meets everything with love and compassion.

So here, for you, a man

Coffee

A coffee circle appeared on the lid of my toilet
How and why it got there is beyond my ken, so I
leave it
Lids on toilets only become tables in important
circumstance
A mug got set down during the peculiar shower
changing of the guard dance
A surprise for her before running out the door,
hot coffee and me
both covenant and symbol, the coffee circle is
held dearly
Like the love it represents it is easily wiped
away
Somehow I nurture it and it persists for another
day

Effort

Leave it all out there
wherever there is
a stage, the meat locker, a warehouse, a
computer, a diner, on the streets, in a hospital, a
ship, a truck, a field
wherever you and duty meet
give it everything
if it is not as natural as a bird taking wing, make
note
be driven by your passion, whether it is for the
means or the end
for that which you pursue and dream, do not
bend

www.ingramcontent.com/pod-product-compliance
Lightning Source LLC
La Vergne TN
LVHW021328200726
843509LV00014B/2436

9 789357 447218